THE CIVIL RIGHTS MOVEMENT

"I say to you today, my friends, so even though we face the difficulties of today and tomorrow, I still have a dream. It is a dream deeply rooted in the American dream. I have a dream that one day this nation will rise up and live out the true meaning of its creed: 'We hold these truths to be self-evident, that all men are created equal.'"

Martin Luther King Jr.

BY ROSE VENABLE

Published by The Child's World®
1980 Lookout Drive, Mankato, MN 56003-1705
800-599-READ • www.childsworld.com

CONTENT CONSULTANT
Kira Duke, Program Manager
National Civil Rights Museum

PHOTOS
Cover and page 4: AP Photo
Interior: AP Photo: 13, 18, 19, 22, 24, 25, 29 (both); AP Photo/Bill Hudson:
17; AP Photo/Chuck Kennedy, Pool: 27; AP Photo/Gene Herrick: 10, 11;
Bettmann via Getty Images: 12; Everett Collection/Newscom: 8, 15; Everett
Collection/Shutterstock.com: 5; Jack Delano/Library of Congress, Prints and
Photographs Division: 6; LBJ Library photo by Yoichi Okamoto: 20; Thomas
J. O'Halloran/Library of Congress, Prints and Photographs Division: 9, 31;
Walter Albertin/Library of Congress, Prints and Photographs Division: 23

LIBRARY OF CONGRESS CATALOGING-IN-PUBLICATION DATA
ISBN 9781503853690 (Reinforced Library Binding)
ISBN 9781503854079 (Portable Document Format)
ISBN 9781503854192 (Online Multi-user eBook)
LCCN: 2020943587

Printed in the United States of America

Cover and page 4 caption:
Dr. Martin Luther King Jr. (hand raised)
marches with thousands in
Alabama on March 21, 1965.

CONTENTS

Chapter One

A CITIZEN'S RIGHTS

For 250 years, even before the United States became a country, slavery was a fact of life throughout the Americas. Africans did not come to the continent by choice. They were brought by slave traders and forced into slavery. It was completely outlawed only after the U.S. Civil War ended, when the Thirteenth **Amendment** to the U.S. **Constitution** was passed in 1865. Black Americans hoped they would finally enjoy freedom and opportunities as U.S. citizens. Even after slavery ended, however, Black people still faced **discrimination** and **injustice**.

People picking cotton in North Carolina in 1900.

In 1940, Black and white people had to wait in separate rooms for their trains at this North Carolina station.

Almost immediately, white people in the southern United States found ways to restrict the rights of Black people. The Fifteenth Amendment to the Constitution guaranteed all Black men the right to vote. It went into effect in February of 1870. (Women of all races could not vote until 1920.) Yet white people in the South found ways to break this law. They did not want Black people to have a say in how the government was run. Sometimes, whites threatened Black people who tried to vote. Whites passed laws stating that people could vote only if they owned property. Black people also had to take a test to prove they could read. However, many Black people were too poor to buy property, and many more could not read. Such laws kept Black people from voting.

Southern states also created **segregation** laws to separate Black people from whites. Laws said that Black people could not eat in the same restaurants, play in the same parks, or drink from the same water fountains as white people. Black children could not go to the same schools as white children. In many places, Black people had to sit in the backs of streetcars and buses and give up their seats to white people.

Northern states had no segregation laws, but that did not mean that Black people were treated fairly. In many places, they were not allowed to buy houses in the same neighborhoods as white people. Black people could not attend the best schools or hold the best jobs. Throughout the country, Black people simply did not have the same opportunities as whites.

Black people were not satisfied with their lives as second-class citizens. Even before slavery ended, many courageous people had begun to fight for equality. By the middle of the twentieth century, a movement had begun in which millions of people worked to win fair treatment for Black people. Because this movement focused on obtaining **civil rights**, many history books call it the civil rights movement. Sometimes it is called the Black freedom movement.

Millions became involved in the civil rights movement—not only adults, but children as well. They held many different kinds of **protests**. In some places, white people became so angry with civil rights protesters that they beat or even killed them.

People disagree on when the civil rights movement began. Some people believe it started when slavery ended in 1865. Others say it started in the early twentieth century. Most sources agree it began in the 1950s. History books often place the end of the movement in 1965 when the Voting Rights Act became law. But other people believe the movement never really ended because Black people continue to fight for equal rights today.

Protestors march against segregated schools in Houston, Texas.

Long before the civil rights movement gained national attention, Black people found ways to fight discrimination. In 1892, a Black shoemaker named Homer Plessy wanted to prove segregation laws were **unconstitutional**. Plessy boarded a train in New Orleans, Louisiana, and sat in a car for white people. As Plessy had expected, he was arrested.

When he went on trial, Plessy argued that segregated railroad cars were unconstitutional. He said they violated the Fourteenth Amendment to the U.S. Constitution, which states that all U.S. citizens have the same rights. Plessy's case made it to the **Supreme Court**. In 1896, the Court decided that Black people could be required to use separate facilities as long as those facilities were equal. This decision became known as the "separate but equal" principle. However, schools, restaurants, and other facilities created for Black people were almost always worse than facilities for whites.

Black people accused of crimes did not always get a fair trial—or any trial at all. Sometimes, white mobs simply assumed Black people were guilty and lynched them before they ever went to court. Many of the people these mobs attacked had committed no crimes.

Injustice stirred more and more Black people to fight for equality. In the early 1900s, a new group formed to fight **racism** and discrimination. It was called the National Association for the Advancement of Colored People (NAACP). Over the years, the NAACP became a powerful organization. By the 1930s, its lawyers were taking cases to court to challenge discrimination. Many of these challenges were successful.

Chapter Two

A MOVEMENT FOR CHANGE

By the 1950s, the NAACP was fighting its most important court case of all: *Brown v. Board of Education*. This case fought segregation in schools. In 1954, the Supreme Court decided that the "separate but equal" law did not apply to schools. It said that segregated schools were illegal according to the U.S. Constitution. Public schools had to be **integrated**. Many consider this decision to be the first major victory of the civil rights movement.

The Supreme Court decision did not immediately end school segregation, however. Many white southerners fought integration. Some white citizens protested outside integrated schools and took their children out of public schools.

A Black teen walks through a crowd of white boys on his way to attend an integrated school in Tennessee.

In 1955, two white men brutally murdered Emmett Till, a 14-year-old Black boy in Mississippi. They killed him because he had supposedly whistled at a white woman. The men accused of Till's murder were arrested. Despite evidence against them, they were found not guilty and set free. Later, they confessed to the murder.

Black people were frustrated that schools were still segregated even after the Supreme Court decision. They realized that the U.S. government could not give them equal rights as quickly as they had hoped. More and more people decided that they had to fight for their rights.

In Montgomery, Alabama, Black people were required by law to ride in the back of public buses. On December 1, 1955, Rosa Parks was on her way home after a long day at work. She took a seat in the middle of the bus. When the bus driver ordered Parks to give up her seat to a white man, she quietly refused. The bus driver called the police, and Parks was arrested.

Parks's action sparked a huge response from Montgomery's Black leaders. The Women's Political Council planned a **boycott** of the buses.

Rosa Parks being fingerprinted after her arrest.

Two ministers, Ralph Abernathy and Martin Luther King Jr., led the community in supporting the boycott. **Activists** printed more than 40,000 flyers to tell Montgomery's Black community about their idea.

The Black residents of Montgomery stopped riding the buses. A few of Montgomery's Black citizens owned cars. They arranged carpools and offered rides to their friends, neighbors, and even to strangers. Some people rode bicycles. Most people walked wherever they needed to go. Some had to walk long distances to work, shopping, or church.

Many white people tried to stop the boycott. Some Black people were fired from their jobs. Bombs were thrown into the houses of King and other NAACP leaders. The protesters were afraid, but they stood firm. The boycott lasted 381 days. Finally, the Supreme Court decided that bus segregation was illegal. Bus segregation ended on December 20, 1956, and the boycott ended the next day.

Rev. Ralph Abernathy (left) shakes hands with Rec. Martin Luther King Jr.

In 1960, four federal officers took six-year-old Ruby Bridges to enroll at a white school in New Orleans, Louisiana. Parents of the white students withdrew their children from the school. For more than a year, Ruby was the only child in her classroom. Finally, white parents sent their children back to the school.

By this time, people around the country knew about the boycott. It made King famous. As the head of a new group called the Southern Christian Leadership Conference (SCLC), King would become the most powerful voice of the civil rights movement. He believed in nonviolent protests such as the boycott. King said protesters should not use violence under any circumstances, even if they were threatened or harmed. The Montgomery bus boycott had shown that nonviolent protests could work.

The boycott inspired Black people to fight for their rights in other places. Even by the end of 1956, there were practically no Black students attending school with white children in the South. When school started in the fall of 1957, nine Black students tried to enroll at Little Rock Central High School in Little Rock, Arkansas.

The governor of Arkansas brought the National Guard to the school to block the students from entering. So President Dwight Eisenhower sent **federal** troops to protect the students and to make sure they could go inside. Finally, Little Rock officials closed the high school for a year so they would not have to integrate it.

Elizabeth Eckford, one of the "Little Rock Nine," ignores the screams and stares of white students as she attends her first day of integrated school.

Chapter Three

THE MOVEMENT GROWS

Civil rights supporters took great pride in the success of the Montgomery bus boycott. They were hopeful when President Eisenhower sent soldiers to help Black students. More and more people joined what was now being called the civil rights movement.

Young people in particular—both Black and white— became involved in the movement. Many believed in the nonviolent protests of Martin Luther King Jr. They used **sit-ins** to fight segregation. They went to restaurants, hotels, parks, and libraries where Black people were not allowed and sat down. When asked to leave, they quietly refused.

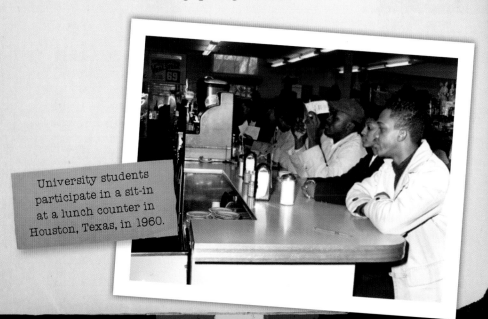

University students participate in a sit-in at a lunch counter in Houston, Texas, in 1960.

Crowds of angry white people came to see the sit-ins. They called the protesters names. Some even attacked the protesters, throwing things or hitting them. When the police came, they arrested the protesters, not the people who had attacked them. Over time, however, sit-ins convinced some businesses to take down their whites-only signs.

Some of the first sit-ins to receive major national press attention took place in Greensboro, North Carolina, in 1960. Four Black students sat at a whites-only lunch counter and refused to leave until they were served. In the following days, hundreds of people joined them. Similar protests soon began across the South.

Young civil rights activists organized groups to fight discrimination. They formed a group called the Congress of Racial Equality (CORE). They also formed a new organization called the Student Nonviolent Coordinating Committee (SNCC). Sometimes SNCC (pronounced SNIK) worked with King's organization. At times, the groups did not agree. King and other older civil rights leaders often wanted to move more slowly than the younger leaders.

In the spring of 1961, college students began another large-scale protest. Members of CORE organized what they called the Freedom Rides. The Supreme Court had decided that bus and railroad stations could not be segregated. Some white southerners did not want to obey this decision. To show the public that discrimination still occurred, Black and white CORE activists rode two buses from Washington, DC to New Orleans, Louisiana.

The first bus trip was difficult for the Freedom Riders. At first, people glared or yelled at them. Then two days into the trip, a young Black Freedom Rider who tried to go into a whites-only waiting room was beaten. A mob threw a bomb into a bus that started a fire and injured its riders.

Freedom Riders in 1961 sit in the Alabama grass after their bus was destroyed by a white mob.

Another mob attacked Freedom Riders in Birmingham, Alabama. Some of the riders were badly hurt. A mob also attacked news reporters who came to cover the Freedom Rides. People everywhere were amazed that the Freedom Riders were willing to face such danger to end discrimination.

For a time, the Freedom Rides stopped. No bus driver would agree to carry the riders. The rides started again after President John F. Kennedy ordered state police to protect the riders. However, the federal government promised not to interfere as long as there was no violence. Local police arrested Freedom Riders, and some went to prison for months.

In 1962, James Meredith applied to the University of Mississippi. When school officials rejected him because he was Black, he took the university to court. The Supreme Court decided in his favor. President Kennedy had to send federal marshals to take Meredith to classes. When a **riot** broke out, two people were killed and approximately 375 people were injured.

Alabama governor George Wallace was against integration. In a speech, Wallace said that the federal government was wrong to fight for civil rights for Black people. In response, an angry President Kennedy called segregation morally wrong in a televised speech. Kennedy's speech encouraged the supporters of the civil rights movement.

More Freedom Riders continued to arrive in the South, and by the end of the summer, more than 300 had been arrested.

The Freedom Riders never made it all the way to New Orleans. Many spent the summer in jail. Some were scarred for life from the beatings they received. But their efforts were not in vain. They forced the Kennedy administration to take a stand on civil rights, which was the Freedom Riders' goal in the first place. In addition, the Interstate Commerce Commission outlawed segregation in interstate bus travel. That ruling took effect in November of 1961. The Freedom Riders may not have finished their trip, but they made an important and lasting contribution to the civil rights movement.

King's organization, the SCLC, began holding marches and sit-ins in Birmingham, Alabama, in the spring of 1963.

On May 2, thousands of schoolchildren took part in one especially large march. T. Eugene "Bull" Connor, the public safety commissioner in Birmingham, sent police to arrest the protesters. Approximately 600 children were sent to jail.

The next day, another march took place. This time, the Birmingham police used high-powered fire hoses to attack the marchers. The force of the water knocked grown men off their feet. Children struck by the water were sent tumbling down the street. When people continued to march, the police brought out dogs and ordered them to attack the marchers—including children.

News cameras captured these terrible events. That night, people all over the world saw what was going on and were outraged. More and more civil rights activists came to Birmingham to show their support for the fight against such injustice. News reporters also came in greater numbers.

White store owners worried that the protesters were making them lose business. They asked the city government to change its segregation laws. Birmingham officials finally agreed. But violence continued in the city as members of a hate group, the **Ku Klux Klan**, bombed Black people's homes and churches.

Police dogs attack 15 year-old Walter Gadsden during a march on May 4, 1963, in Birmingham, Alabama.

Chapter Four

"I HAVE A DREAM"

In a 1963 speech, President Kennedy promised to push a civil rights bill through Congress. He said he would introduce a bill making it illegal to discriminate against anyone because of race. Civil rights leaders considered this a major victory. But the very night Kennedy delivered his speech, civil rights leader Medgar Evers was killed in Jackson, Mississippi.

The death of Evers made it clear that the civil rights movement still had much to accomplish. To convince Congress to pass President Kennedy's bill, civil rights leaders organized the March on Washington. On August 28, 1963, approximately 250,000 people of all races and from all over the nation came to show their support.

Medgar Evers's widow comforts their son at the funeral.

One of the most memorable moments of this inspiring day took place when Martin Luther King Jr. delivered a stirring speech to the crowd. He summed up his hopes for the United States.

"I have a dream that my four little children will one day live in a nation where they will not be judged by the color of their skin but by the content of their character. I have a dream today!"

The March on Washington inspired people all over the country. Many people were encouraged to make life better for Black people. However, some white people were still committed to stopping them.

In September of 1963, a bomb was planted at a Black church in Birmingham, Alabama. Four little girls attending Sunday school were killed. People again expressed outrage and sorrow. And yet some members of Congress still would not vote for a civil rights law.

On November 22, 1963, President John Kennedy was **assassinated**. Vice President Lyndon Johnson became the new president.

Martin Luther King Jr. gives his "I Have a Dream" speech in Washington DC on August 28, 1963.

President Lyndon Johnson shakes Martin Luther King Jr's hand after signing the 1964 Civil Rights Act.

Ku Klux Klan member Byron De La Beckwith was arrested shortly after the murder of Medgar Evers but was found not guilty in two separate trials. For years, Myrlie Evers tried to put her husband's murderer behind bars. In 1994, Beckwith was finally found guilty of murdering Medgar Evers and sentenced to life in prison.

At first, civil rights leaders worried that Kennedy's law would never become reality. But Johnson shared the dream of equality. He pushed Congress to pass the Civil Rights Act of 1964. This law outlawed segregation in all public places. It allowed the U.S. government to make schools integrate. When Johnson signed the bill on July 2, it was a major victory for the civil rights movement.

Members of the movement were still fighting another form of discrimination: restriction of voting rights. Civil rights leaders knew that if more Black people voted, they would have more say in the government. They wanted to register more Black people to vote.

In 1963, voter registration drives had begun in Mississippi, Alabama, and Georgia. In the summer of 1964, student volunteers from the North traveled to Mississippi. Many of these young people were white. They planned a massive voter registration drive called Freedom Summer. Three of these activists disappeared and were later found dead. They had been kidnapped and murdered for helping Black people register to vote.

In March of 1965, civil rights leaders held a large protest in Selma, Alabama. Thousands of Black people went to the Selma courthouse to take the voter registration test. The sheriff had them arrested. Some protesters were beaten. The protesters planned a march to Montgomery, Alabama's capital, on March 7. Police officers on horseback clubbed and beat the protesters. The attacks appeared on televisions all over the country. People were horrified at the events that took place on "Bloody Sunday."

In 1964, SNCC members started what they called Freedom Schools. These schools taught Black people to read and write so they could pass the tests required to vote.

Two days later, protesters continued the march. But police again arrived to stop them. That night, one minister who had joined the protest was badly beaten. He later died from his wounds. People from across the country, Black and white, demanded that another law be passed to protect voting rights. President Johnson worked to persuade Congress to pass a voting rights law.

Johnson kept his promise. On March 15, eight days after "Bloody Sunday," he introduced the bill to Congress. On March 21, King organized another march. He led marchers on a five-day journey from Selma to Montgomery. This time federal troops stood by to protect them.

As the protesters marched, more and more people joined them. By the time they reached Montgomery, the marchers were 25,000 strong.

That summer, on August 6, the president signed the Voting Rights Act of 1965. This law required the national government to supervise voter registration in the South. Within a month after the Voting Rights Act passed, one quarter of a million Black people registered to vote for the first time. Between 1964 and 1968, the number of Black voters in the South increased from 1 million to 3.1 million.

Marchers cross the Alabama River at Selma on March 21, 1965, at the start of their five-day march to Montgomery.

Chapter Five

THE CHANGING CIVIL RIGHTS MOVEMENT

After Black people began to vote in greater numbers in the South, Martin Luther King Jr. talked about new goals for the civil rights movement. The movement had focused on change in the South and had accomplished great things. King wanted to help Black people in northern states fight racism as well.

Throughout the nation, Black people still lacked the opportunities whites enjoyed. A government committee created by President Johnson described the United States as "a nation moving toward two societies—one Black, one white, separate and unequal." Civil rights protests began in the North, but change was slow to come.

Martin Luther King Jr. speaks at a press conference in 1964.

Malcolm X holds up a paper for people to see at a New York rally in 1963.

Some young Black people questioned King's goals and his methods. They did not share his belief that the United States would be fully integrated one day. They thought civil rights workers should fight back if attacked. They followed another leader, Malcolm X. For years, Malcolm X had said that Black people should fight back to gain power. He also said that Black people should not work for integration. Instead, he believed the races should remain separate. Malcolm X was assassinated in February of 1965. His views became increasingly popular among activists frustrated by slow progress.

Some Black people in the North felt that the civil rights movement had not helped them. They had never faced segregation laws. Few had experienced difficulty trying to vote. Yet many lived in inner-city slums, trapped by poverty. The civil rights movement had not addressed these issues as strongly.

In the summer of 1965, just five days after President Johnson signed the Voting Rights Act, race riots broke out in Los Angeles, California. Tensions had finally boiled over from longstanding frustrations in the Black community over high unemployment rates and inadequate schools and housing. Over the next six days, 50,000 Black people took to the streets, stealing from shops, setting fire to white-owned businesses, and shooting law officers. By the end of the riots, 34 people had been killed, 1,000 hurt, and 4,000 arrested. Riots followed in Chicago, Illinois, and in Springfield, Massachusetts. More race riots took place the following summer.

Demonstrators in Los Angeles, California, overwhelm a police car during the 1965 race riots.

On April 4, 1968, Martin Luther King Jr. was assassinated in Memphis, Tennessee. People of all races mourned his death. Afterward, people disagreed even further about how to fight for equality.

Young Black people had begun to talk about a new Black Power movement. Those involved were angry that racism still existed even after the tremendous efforts of civil rights activists in the 1950s and 1960s. Black Power supporters agreed with Malcolm X's belief that Black people needed to be completely independent from whites. Some formed a new group called the Black Panther Party.

Black Panther members believed that Black protesters should defend themselves when demonstrations became violent—even if that meant using violence themselves. Some Black Panthers were killed in fights with police officers. Others went to prison. By the late 1960s, many people said the civil rights movement had ended. However, groups such as the Black Panthers continued to fight for equality, justice, and opportunity.

Black people in the United States had gained important victories during the civil rights movement. Legal segregation no longer existed. Black people in the South could now vote. Black leaders began to win elections and take part in local, state, and national government. However, many important leaders in the movement had been killed, including Medgar Evers, Malcolm X, and Martin Luther King Jr. And although much had been gained, much work was still left to be done.

In 2008 Barack Obama was elected the first Black president of the United States. His election showed the country had improved somewhat since the civil rights movement and inspired hope that discrimination and racism would continue to decrease. But protests and anger swelled nationwide in 2020 following the deaths of numerous Black men and women at the hands of police.

Although people everywhere express great pride in the achievements of the civil rights movement, discrimination and **prejudice** still keep the United States from being a land truly dedicated to freedom. People continue to fight racism and discrimination, seeking justice and opportunity for all.

In 2012, a Black 17-year-old named Trayvon Martin was shot and killed by a white man, George Zimmerman. In 2013, a jury declared Zimmerman not-guilty. In response, three Black organizers, Alicia Garza, Patrisse Cullors, and Opal Tometi, created the hashtag #BlackLivesMatter and set off a movement for freedom, liberation, and justice that continues today.

Barack Obama stands with his wife and daughters as he is sworn in as president of the United States on January 20, 2009.

Explain the ways that young people played a part in the Civil Rights Movement.
Why was their support important?

During the lunch counter sit-ins, the police arrested the Black silent protesters.
They also turned fire hoses on Black marchers in Birmingham.
How might a history of police support of white people over Black
affect the relationship between the police and Black people today?

TIME LINE

1890-1910

1896
The Supreme Court decides in *Plessy v. Ferguson* that segregation is legal as long as Black people have access to equal facilities. This ruling becomes known as the "separate but equal" principle.

1909
The National Association for the Advancement of Colored People (NAACP) is founded.

1950

1954
The Supreme Court decides in *Brown v. Board of Education* that public schools cannot be segregated.

1955
In August, two white men murder Emmett Till in Mississippi. In December, Rosa Parks is arrested in Alabama, after refusing to give up her bus seat to a white man. Black community leaders plan a boycott to protest segregation on buses.

1956
The Supreme Court decides that bus segregation is illegal. The Montgomery bus boycott ends on December 20.

1957
Black students are barred from enrolling at a public high school in Little Rock, Arkansas. After the federal government says Black students must be allowed to enroll, Little Rock closes the school rather than admit Black people. Martin Luther King Jr. founds a new civil rights organization, the Southern Christian Leadership Conference (SCLC).

1960

1960
The first major sit-in takes place in North Carolina.

1961
Young activists known as Freedom Riders ride buses from Washington DC to New Orleans.

1962
James Meredith tries to enroll at the University of Mississippi. After the Supreme Court declares that he must be admitted, a riot occurs in which two people die and many more are hurt.

Photos, such as the one on page 17, helped bring support to the Civil Rights Movement.
Why do you think that is?

Throughout history, white people made it difficult for Black people to buy houses in certain neighborhoods, go to school with white kids, or vote.
Why is it important that Black people have the same opportunities as white people?
What happens when they do not?

2000s

1963
Civil rights leaders begin registering new voters in the South. On June 12, President John F. Kennedy promises that Congress will pass a civil rights bill. That same night, civil rights activist Medgar Evers is murdered. The March on Washington takes place on August 28. In September, four little girls are killed in a church bombing in Birmingham, Alabama. In November, President Kennedy is assassinated.

1964
Student volunteers travel to Mississippi to organize voter registration drives. Three volunteers are kidnapped and murdered. The Civil Rights Act becomes law on July 2.

1965
Police attack civil rights protesters at a march in Selma, Alabama. President Lyndon Johnson signs the Voting Rights Act into law on August 6, protecting the right of all U.S. citizens to vote.

1966
The Black Power movement begins.

1968
Martin Luther King Jr. is assassinated on April 4.

2008
Barack Obama is elected the first Black president of the United States on November 4.

2020
After the deaths of numerous Black men and women at the hands of police, protests are held all over the world to raise awareness about racism and discrimination.

activists (AK-tiv-ists)
Activists are people who take strong action to support a view or belief. Civil rights activists worked to achieve better treatment for Black people.

amendment (uh-MEND-munt)
An amendment is a change made to a law or an official document. An amendment to the U.S. Constitution ended slavery.

assassinated (uh-SASS-uh-nayt-ed)
When an important or famous person has been murdered, he or she has been assassinated. Several civil rights leaders were assassinated.

boycott (BOY-kot)
A boycott is a protest in which people stop using a certain product or service. A bus boycott helped end segregation on public buses in Montgomery, Alabama.

civil rights (SIV-ul RYTZ)
Civil rights are a person's rights to freedom and equal treatment. The civil rights movement focused on winning equal treatment for Black people.

Constitution (kon-stuh-too-shun)
The Constitution is the written document containing the principles by which the United States is governed.

discrimination (dis-krim-uh-NAY-shun
Discrimination is the unfair treatment of people because of their race, religion, sex, or other characteristics. Even after slavery ended, Black people struggled against discrimination.

federal (FED-ur-ull)
Federal means having to do with the nation's central government rather than a state or local government. In 1960, four federal officers took Ruby Bridges to enroll at a white school.

injustice (in-JUSS-tiss)
Injustice is something that is unfair or wrong. People who are denied equal rights are victims of injustice.

integrated (IN-tuh-gray-ted)
If something is integrated, all people can use it equally. In 1954, the Supreme Court declared that all public schools must be integrated.

Ku Klux Klan (KOO KLUKS KLAN)
The Ku Klux Klan is a hate group that believes white people of certain religions are better than other people. The Ku Klux Klan has committed many acts of violence against Black people and other people.

lynched (LINCHD)
When a person is lynched, they are put to death—often by hanging—by a mob. Some Black people in the South were lynched for crimes they did not commit.

prejudice (PREJ-uh-diss)
Prejudice is a bad feeling or opinion about something or someone without good reason. Prejudice is a problem in the United States.

protests (PROH-tests)
Protests are public statements or gatherings in which people speak out to say something is wrong. Activists held many kinds of protests during the civil rights movement.

racism (RAY-sih-zum)
Racism is a negative feeling or opinion about people because of their race. The NAACP was formed to fight all forms of racism.

riot (RY-ut)
A riot is public violence by a large group of people. Five days after the Voting Rights Act was signed, riots broke out in Los Angeles.

segregation (seh-gruh-GAY-shun)
Segregation is the practice of using laws to keep people apart. Segregation separated Black people and whites in the South for many years.

sit-ins (SIT-inz)
Sit-ins are a protest in which people sit down and refuse to leave. During the civil rights movement, sit-ins helped end segregation in restaurants.

Supreme Court (suh-PREEM KORT)
The Supreme Court is the most powerful court in the United States. A Supreme Court decision ended school segregation.

unconstitutional (un-kon-stuh-TOO-shun-ul)
If something is unconstitutional, it is not allowed by the U.S. Constitution. Homer Plessy wanted to prove that segregation laws were unconstitutional.

BOOKS

Asim, Jabari. *A Child's Introduction to African American History: The Experiences, People, and Events That Shaped Our Country*. New York, NY: Black Dog & Leventhal, 2018.

Clark-Robinson, Monica. *Let the Children March*. Solon, OH: Findaway World, 2019.

Evans, Shane W. *We March*. New York, NY: Square Fish, 2016.

Hooks, Gwendolyn. *If You Were a Kid During the Civil Rights Movement*. New York, NY: Children's Press, 2017.

Osborne, Linda Barrett. *Miles to Go for Freedom: Segregation and Civil Rights in the Jim Crow Years*. New York, NY: Abrams Books for Young Readers, 2012.

Tonatiuh, Duncan. *Separate Is Never Equal: Sylvia Mendez and Her Family's Fight for Desegregation*. New York, NY: Abrams Books for Young Readers, 2014.

WEBSITES

Visit our website for links about the Civil Rights Movement:

childsworld.com/links

Note to Parents, Teachers, and Librarians: We routinely verify our Web links to make sure they are safe, active sites—so encourage your readers to check them out!

INDEX